The Evil Supreme Court

The Evil Supreme Court

✦

A TREATISE—ON WHY THE OVERTURN OF THE ANDERSEN CONVICTION IS WRONG.

Walter F. Picca

iUniverse, Inc.

New York Lincoln Shanghai

The Evil Supreme Court
A TREATISE—ON WHY THE OVERTURN OF THE ANDERSEN CONVICTION IS WRONG.

iUniverse books may be ordered through booksellers or by contacting:

iUniverse
2021 Pine Lake Road, Suite 100
Lincoln, NE 68512
www.iuniverse.com
1-800-Authors (1-800-288-4677)

ISBN-13: 978-0-595-36670-5 (pbk)
ISBN-13: 978-0-595-81091-8 (ebk)
ISBN-10: 0-595-36670-8 (pbk)
ISBN-10: 0-595-81091-8 (ebk)

Printed in the United States of America

Contents

Foreword

The Evil Supreme Court was first published in July, 2005, as attachment # 3—added to **The Story of the New Valley Corporation Common Shareholder Lawsuit**—and republished as a separate book by iUniverse Publishing Services.

Dissenting opinion

I am referring to the May 31, 2005 unanimous ruling of the Supreme Court—that overturned the criminal conviction of Arthur Andersen.

I called five of the Supreme Court justices idiots for not finding the sentencing of Leandro Andrade 25 years to life—twice for two K–Mart video thefts—totaling $153—as cruel and unusual.

Now, I am calling all nine supreme court justices idiots—for ignoring a mountain of hard evidence—and overturning the Andersen conviction on a bogus technicality: the jury instructions were flawed.

Asking the head of Arthur Andersen or senior officers whether they intended to commit a crime by what they did—is not reason for overturning a ruling; generally, most guilty people, will deny their guilt—at an investigation—to avoid prosecution, jail, etc.—and in this case, (also) protect themselves from civil lawsuits.

Of course, there was a deliberate obstruction of justice. The trouble in Enron surfaced in October 16, 2001–it was all over the new—nationally. Andersen, externally and internally, seen the investigation coming. Days later, truck loads of documents were destroyed and tens of thousand of emails were deleted. This all took place until November the 9th—the day SEC requested Andersen's records relating to Enron. It was not a routine disposal of old, irrelevant documents. This is proof of intent—to impede, subvert—or obstruct a federal investigation.

How, can anybody deny this.

This ruling of the Supreme Court is a slap in the face—of the jury that seen the evidence during a 4 month trial—and deliberated 10 days—and found the auditing firm—guilty of obstructing justice.

The Supreme Court ruling—based on flaws, they say: in the judge's instructions—overrides—two tons of evidence.

This so–called flaw—or phony excuse—no ways, outweighs the fact they destroyed tons evidence—days before the investigation—hit the door—is sufficient proof of evil intent—to cover up their involvement in the fraudulent accounting scandal that surfaced—at Enron. What the Supreme Court wants us to accept; even though, Andersen obstructed justice by ordering the destruction of the Enron documents—because the faulty jury instructions: the guilty verdict should be annulled. The ruling: they were wrongly convicted—because of faulty jury instructions—is preposterous.

I can assure you—that each member of the Supreme Court—did not look at all the evidence at the trial. That would have taken too much time. The twelve jurors—were the better judges.

The lawyers for the defendant—were looking for a small flaw—in the case, and the (pressured) Supreme Court finally agreed. It shows the power of the oligarchs—even, over the Supreme Court.

It shows: the rich and powerful—after convictions: can hire top–paid lawyers to pester (or pressure) the courts with one argument after another—until they find a bias judge that agrees.

Remember back in the S & L scandal: Charles Keating's conviction was overturned; because the court ruled: the judge allowed the jury to convict him without determined whether he intended to defraud investors. They want the verdict to be based on intent—something intangible, rather than factual. It is similar to the excuse: the Supreme Court used to overturn

Andersen's conviction: the jury instructions failed to require the necessary proof that Andersen knew it actions were wrong—this is ludicrous.

Here is how it works: the lawyers wait—until the public anger dies down—or forgets. Then, they try to spring their rich convicted clients, on a technicality (when nobody is watching). I would venture to say: that every conviction of an US executive—is on appeal—like, not one believes he was fairly convicted by US courts. And they have the money to hire the best lawyers that hammer away until they get results—in most cases.

I don't have to the time to check all cases. But, a study should be made—to see if, there is a pattern—of reducing and overturning sentences of rich and powerful people (or executives) convicted of crimes—on minor technicalities (or perceived flaws) somewhere in the legal proceedings.

The junk–bond king Michael Milken—served only 22 months of a ten–year sentence after pleading guilt to securities fraud—to avoid a worst charge (after thousands of investors lost millions of dollars). While, there are thousands of men and women in prison—serving near life terms—for petty crimes. The Supreme Court looked at both these cases: Andrade and Andersen: and ruled unfairly: in both cases. It is an obvious, glaring injustice: in two opposites extremes: strict law enforcement for the street criminals—and little or no justice for corporate executives: the rich political donor class. The US Supreme Court made two big mistakes.

Of course, the accounting procedures used by Enron were unsound and fraudulent. And, Andersen signed off on these Annual Reports—that were false and misleading. The Annual Report did not represent the true picture of the company's financial condition. Naturally, they wanted all documents destroyed—before the investigation got started, in which shareholders and investors lost billions of dollars.

They failed to serve the purpose of an auditor: an independent look at the corporation's facts and figures—to see if there is no misrepresentation—which they failed to do. They were playing ball with Enron.

That is why Arthur Anderson—was so successful. He knew the all the accounting methods, got in bed with executives, overlooked their off–the–book activities (schemes), provided corporate tax–evading strategies, condoned "illegal transaction", mixed auditing with consulting, would not reveal company secrets, and destroyed incriminating documents—when necessary. I would not believe him—if, he said: he did not. And he would say to the press: I did nothing wrong.

If, the SEC appointed auditors—instead of being chosen by the corporations—there would be different results. That would make manipulating the books a lot harder to accomplish. Today—some have become too lax—and do not serve the purpose of an auditor—to look for inaccuracies—and misrepresentations (to protect investors). Their loyalty is to executives.

In choosing an accounting firm: honest and accurate bookkeeping is not the main concern for corporations: computers can do that. What is important—avoiding the corporate income tax—and if necessary—portray a healthy image of the corporation—when it is not—to maintain or inflate stock prices. Here is where the big money is made—creative accounting methods.

Enron paid no income tax in four of the last five years: despite a $1.8 billion in reported US profits. You ask, how can that be done. Well, Andersen, who does consulting and tax services—along side auditing, can probably show you how to make US based corporation profits show up in the books of foreign subsidiaries—where there is no corporate income tax—called tax havens: Enron had almost 900. In fact, we know: today: that Anderson: helped to design the off–the–book schemes that lead to the demise of Enron, and gave its seal of approval to Enron financial statements. I would not believe Arthur Andersen, if he said: he didn't. And I would not believe—if, he said—I did nothing (wrong).

Ten major strikes

One: Arthur Anderson settled a civil case—for $217 million stemming from the collapse of the Baptist Foundation of Arizona. Anderson was accused of concealing losses on financial statements related to its auditing of the foundation: prices plummeted—and investors and employees lost billions.

Two: Anderson was also involved in fraudulent and auditing practices at Sunbeam, which went bankrupt: Anderson settled a lawsuit with Shareholders out of Court: $110 million.

Three: Anderson agreed to pay a $7 million fine for issuing false and misleading reports on behalf of Waste Management, Inc.—and part of a $229 million settlement with shareholders.

Four: Asia Pulp and Paper Company defaulted on $6 billion in bonds: Arthur Andersen, the parent company's auditor.

Five: Andersen was involved in fraudulent accounting and auditing practices at WorldCom—and settled for $65 million.

Six: A New York jury found Andersen negligent in approving favorable, but not accurate figures for the Delorean Motor Company, which went bankrupt, and awarded the bankruptcy trustee—nearly $100 million—before they settled, presumably for less.

Seven: Andersen paid $90 million to bilked investors for signing off on overly rosy forecasts for Colonial Realty.

Eight: Anderson was among those blamed for the S & L scandal back in the 1980s.

Nine: Andersen paid $5.5 million to cover taxpayers losses at the failed Home Savings Bank, rather than face charges: it was negligent in reviewing its books.

Ten: Andersen's involvement in the fraudulent accounting and auditing scandal at Enron—the $100 billion implosion.

And there were others: Qwest, Peregine, Dynegy, etc. Anderson was also the auditor for **Global Crossing.**

It was, once, a reputable accounting firm—one of the Big Five—and got increasing greedy and unethical—and after Andersen's conviction—lost it licenses to audit public corporations (and deceased).

I empathize with innocent Anderson employees—who lost their jobs—but not for the corrupt Arthur Anderson partners. But, I empathize more for the Enron shareholders, small investors, and employees—who lost billions.

Of course, Arthur Andersen, knowingly obstructed justice by destroying related Enron documents and that made it harder—or nearly impossible to prosecute the Enron Executives (and prove Andersen's involvement)—along with—the use of Fifth Amendment—by Andersen and Enron executives.

Andersen was smart enough—that if, there was no culpatory information in these Enron documents—they would never been destroyed. They would have been preserved for his defense. That was not the case—there was incriminating evidence in these documents, and why they were destroyed—and could not have happened without his knowing about it—or ordering it. It was not a co–incident—the federal government came with subpoenas—while they were shredding documents. What was at stake here: the firm's survival, costly civil litigation (avoidance), criminal prosecution of himself and his Enron auditing team—and possibly Enron executives: that was the motive—for the orchestrated and hurried house cleaning.

Anyways, the Supreme Court should have waited to see what facts come to light—in the trial of the Enron executives—before exonerating Andersen. It acted prematurely. When the full truth is known: the Supreme Court will look like the Ship of Fools.

Justice Antonin Scalia—called—the government's theory of the case: "weird". It is not weird at all. What is weird: his statement. This is an attempt—to smirch a good and just jury verdict—and give back a good name to a convicted felon—a comrade. He does not think—anybody should go to jail for destroying tons of Enron related documents: that would help get to the bottom of the Enron collapse—in which, tens of thousands of people lost their jobs, some employees their life–savings, and investors and shareholders: billions. He is pal of the President—a member of the plutocracy. He is loyal to the oligarchs, his friends—not the people (or victims of fraud). He wants to make it harder to investigate and prosecute corporate crime. His view: this was a routine disposal of old and unneeded Enron related documents: a 1% possibility out of 99.

However, he does think—one should spend: fifty years to life in prison—for stealing $153 worth of videos: that he voted to uphold. He is twice an idiot—and probably more.

Chief Justice Rehnquist (writing the opinion of the court) nixes the Andersen jury verdict claiming: the judge's instructions to the jury were flawed. But, what is flawed: his reasoning. It is not necessary to prove whether the Anderson's top–level management believed what they did was wrong—what they say—is not reliable proof, as what they did under the circumstances. They could not help, but know—that the destruction of Enron documents was to head–off a Federal probe—and that (some) of these document were damaging to Anderson and Enron and some of top executives (involved).

Chief Justice Rehnquist's—reasoning—shows a certain degree of mental loss—or even insanity by rejecting the verdict of Arthur Andersen—now—all his rulings are suspect. If, he is lunatic in one case, he probably is in others. And I will explain that in a few minutes.

And what I said about Pope John the II, and Arafat—is true of the 80–year–old Rehnquist: he should retire before he is becomes entirely incompetent.

The fact, Rehnquist has cancer of the throat—should say something: if, you believed (some) diseases—are manifestations of mental states (or character): I am inclined to think there is a connection (here).

Maybe, this is a sign—he speaks wrongly.

Read all about it—

I read the FrontPage story of the Supreme Court ruling voiding the Andersen conviction. In the NY Times, the Los Angeles Times, and the Wall Street Journal—and there was no condemnation; most the opinions voiced were positive: the corporate bars welcomed the news. The NY Times said: There were rumblings among former Andersen partners and some legal analysts that this was proof that the accounting firm should never have been indicted, much less found guilty. And at the top of the page—there is an old picture of Andersen employees holding up placards—condemning the prosecution of Andersen—outrageous, punishment of the innocent, etc. Let me first start—by saying: yes it is sad: that after the conviction of Arthur Andersen—on obstruction of justice—the firm lost its licenses—and many people lost their jobs. But, look—the US Justice Department—is the not the culprit. The management of Andersen is at fault. It was one of the top five accounting firms—but, after Arthur Andersen, its founder died—and new management took over and it became increasingly more greedy and unethical—until it self-destructed. If, it had followed the motto—of Arthur Andersen—"Think straight, talk straight"—this would have never happened. Enron was one of its major clients. But, what had happened—Andersen failed in its primary function—to make sure—the financial statements to shareholders and investors were accurate, but they won't. Profits and assets—were misrepresented. And Arthur Andersen was the auditor: and it failed—miserably. The books were doctored to convey a false image of Enron—to inflate its stock on Wall Street. When the hoax was exposed to the public—the company begin to fall apart. Unlike Enron: Andersen was a limited liability partnership—it had no shares—there was no looting of the company by the officers—as was—in the case of Enron. They dumped their shares—as the price was plummeting—while painting a picture—the company was in good shape—it wasn't. This was the bigger disaster: shareholders, employees, and investors lost billions And, Andersen—was partly to blame—it signed off on shareholder reports, where the stated profits and asset were bogus. They were in collusion with Enron. The primary purpose of auditing—is to make sure—a company's financial statements are accurate and true. In the case of Enron—they are not. Therefore, the position: the NY times, The Los Angeles Times, and the Wall Street Journal took—seem to be on the side of Andersen, the corporate defense lawyers, and the Supreme Court. They represented the voices of the oligarchs. They failed to represents the victims of fraud. I don't think the shareholders and employees of the Enron scandal—think it was fair and good ruling. Or would the jurors think—that changing the wording of the jury instructions would have made any difference in their verdict. Andersen—destroyed Enron documents—not because these documents were old and no longer necessary—but to cover its involvement—in the fraudulent accounting procedures—used at Enron—to inflate stock prices. Their actions—proves evil intent. Therefore, the conclusion of the Supreme Courts that the US prosecution of Andersen—was unfair and failed to prove Andersen and its senior officer were conscious of wrongdoing—is ludicrous.

One flaw cited by Rehnquist: the jury was advised that Andersen officials could be guilty of acting: "corruptly" even if, they "honestly and sincerely believed" their conduct was legal. I will tell you why that is not necessarily bad. Few guilty people—tell the truth—facing an indictment. I believe, what they did is proof of intent—not what they say they believed. The CEO testified it was not authorized. That is very unlikely—so I don't believe it. I believe the evidence. CEO of Andersen and senior officers—refused to testify under oath (at the trial). So, that little flaw is irrelevant here: and I don't believe what they said. And, without doubt, they knew these documents—were incriminating. That is why they were shredded. To—protect themselves against criminal prosecution and civil lawsuits. If, the documents—contained no incriminating evidence—they would have kept them—to exculpate themselves—from the scandal. Innocent people did not destroy documents—that would prove their innocence—they preserved them. Are there any incidences in the past, where mid and low level employees—rushed to shred tons of Andersen documents—without top–level authorization. No.

The justices ruled the US District judge should have instructed the jury that the law required the government to prove the Andersen knew it was breaking the law. I will tell why that is faulty—it requires getting into the mind—making more important what a person thinks—than does. Naturally, people will lie faced with criminal prosecution. And in the Andersen case: senior offices took the Fifth; so, we don't know what they thought. But, we know what they did—facing an imminent official investigation.

The nine Supreme Court justices must have overlooked the fact: that Andersen's partner—David B. Duncan pleaded guilty to the obstruction of justice. And, undoubtedly—he conferred with partners at Houston and higher–ups. This matter—was too important—that they would not consult each other—before taking action of this magnitude. But, they won't talk—or admit it. Where in Arthur Andersen's motto—does it say: "don't talk—talk falsely." Therefore, it is unreasonable for the Supreme Court—to overturn the conviction—simply on the bases of this so–called flaw. It tends to make conviction base on proving what a person believes—rather than what they did. Look at how many people have pleaded not guilty—and have been convicted.

Timeline

2001: October 12: Nancy Temple, an Andersen lawyer in Chicago—Anderson's headquarters: emails a letter to its Houston partners and officers: reminding them of the company's document retention policy: it is believed this letter—prompted the wholesale destruction of the Enron documents and deletion of computer files—or was a get ready—alert.

2001: October 16: Enron announced a third–quarter loss of $618: and later that day—or next: its shareholder net equity would be reduced by $1.2 billion. This is when the accounting scandal at Enron—first surfaced. Enron was an elaborate accounting hoax—in part. The previous reported profits and assets were overstated. They were based on mark–to–market equities gains—to puff up stock prices. Now, the truth comes to light—they were not from legitimate business operations. They were from off–balance sheet "special purpose entities"—dubbed the Raptors. They had different purposes: one—to enrich executives. To solve the developing crisis—Enron used it shares to off set losses in its off–the–books partnerships—when the price of the Enron shares fell: the Raptors backfired—and profits and assets vanished. The Raptors began collapsing like floors in the Twin Towers. Assets were converted into liabilities and become heavier and heavier—as the price of Enron shares continued to fall. That spells big trouble—for Andersen—Enron's consultant and auditor. These "special purpose entities"—were base on unsound and fraudulent accounting principles. They are kept off the balance sheet—so, shareholders and investors could not see them. When the news broke—there was a tumultuous uproar, so the government was forced to action.

2001: October 19: Enron alerted the Andersen audit team: that the SEC has begun an inquiry into Enron's off–balance sheet "special purpose entities"—called the Raptors. This must have frightened Andersen, because, the next morning: there was an emergency conference call among high–level Andersen management: to address the situation. It was decided that documents related to the investigation was to be assembled.

2002 October 22: David B. Duncan—in charge of the Houston headquarters auditing team, instead of preserving the documentation to assist Enron and the SEC investigation—orders the immediate shredding of tons of Enron documents in different places: including: Portland Oregon, London England, and Chicago—Andersen's headquarters—according to the indictment.

2001: October 23: David B. Duncan organizes a meeting—to speed up the document destruction—according to managing director: Dorsey Lee Baskin Jr.

2001: November 8: the SEC served Enron and Andersen with subpoenas to provide documents, etc.

2001: November 9: Nancy Temple sends an email—to David B. Duncan and five others: to "stop the shredding." This E–mail is very specific: describes Andersen's retention policy in detail. Not, like the first. If, the first was stated like the second—there would be no destruction. The beginning and the end—of shredding came from an email from the Chicago headquarters. Do you think—she ordered (and stopped) the shredding—without authorization. She does not have to answer questions about private communications with the head of Andersen—or senior officers—that is protected by attorney–client privilege. And in the trial—she refused to testify. She is Andersen's deep–throat. Orders, messages, and alerts were transmitted through her. If, she was indicted: not that I think she should take the blame for Andersen; but she might crack—and give up names. If, she is listening: I would like to tell her—there is nothing more important that she can do in this life: than tell the truth. And show what complete fools—the Supreme Court is. But, I don't think she will be prosecuted. The Attorney General is appointed by Bush Jr.—who is a liar—himself, and made big money in questionable business deals—and is in–tight with the oligarchs. He does not want to embarrass his friends on the Supreme Court—and Andersen was the fourth biggest donor to his presidential campaign.

2001: November 29: the SEC begins investigating Arthur Andersen (concerning the Enron fiasco).

2001: December 2: Enron files for bankruptcy—largely brought about by unsound and fraudulent accounting procedures—called "Raptors"—off–balance sheet partnerships that hide or misrepresent the companies profits, assets, and liabilities, and which (some) executive made personal profits. The purpose of an auditor—is to detect and destroy unsound and fraudulent accounting artifices—not to go along with (or overlook). In addition to that: we know today: Andersen co–designed (some) Raptors—and approved an unsound solution, that violated accounting rules, to shore up those—that were impaired: that, eventually—led to the collapse of Enron. The full truth is yet to be unraveled. That is why Andersen wanted a quick trial—before the facts became known. Kenneth Lay blames Andersen.

2002: January 10: Andersen states that it destroyed Enron Documents.

Between October 22 and November 9, 2001: tons of Enron's related document were destroyed working overtime using dozens of trucks and over ten thousand emails deleted.

This behemoth undertaking in different places throughout the United States and the world could not be done without the CEO of Andersen, partners and senior officers—discussing, approving and supervising it. They can deny it—and refused to testify—but is it not possible—or believable.

2002: April 9: David B. Duncan pleaded guilty and stated: "Documents were in fact destroyed so that they would not be available to SEC," he told the US district judge: Melinda Harmon. What—more proof—do you need. There is more:

The October 16, 2001 email sent by Temple: that requested a memorandum be amended—or language deleted, in which David B. Duncan advised Enron not to release the October 19th bad earnings news—or the release was misleading. Enron did, anyways. Temple also requested her name be deleted from the email and refused to testify at the trial. David

Duncan altered the document. It was viewed—as an attempt to keep information from the SEC and obscure the financial condition of Enron. This was a crucial piece of evidence to some jurors.

2002: June 15: Anderson was found guilty of obstruction of justice.

2004, July 1: The 5th District Court of Appeals in New Orleans—upheld the Arthur Andersen conviction.

Did the nine members of the Supreme Court review the evidence—or facts: or read the Grand Jury charges and the indictment: I did and found:

The evidence was sufficient to convict.

And the bogus excuse used by the Supreme Court—was woefully insufficient to overturn the verdict. The shredding of the tons of documents was deliberate—and somebody—higher up—approved it—or gave the go–ahead. And David B Duncan is not the only perpetrator. He is the scapegoat.

2005 May 31—the guilty conviction was overturned by the Supreme Court—in an unanimous decision.

It is a really; big set back for man, when the Supreme Court in an important case—comes down on the side—of the plundering corporate plutocracy—and exonerated a convicted felon—so Andersen can restart its notorious auditing, consulting, and corporate tax services. Enron robbed the bank; Arthur Andersen drove the get–away–car.

The Supreme Court made two bad rulings:

The rejecting of the Arthur Anderson verdict—and the approval of the unjust sentences of thousands of California inmates—serving 25 years to life in prison—for petty crimes. The Supreme Court—intervened—to save one member of the plutocracy; a big party donor, but not for thousands of men and woman—unjustly sentenced in California.

Actually, I think, the Supreme Court should have—went in the opposite direction—solidified the conviction. The petitioner's arguments were flawed. They claimed the jury was never allowed to hear the full truth behind the case. The real reason, why: senior officers refused to testify. Andersen blames the government: for the Andersen's employees that lost their jobs: They claim there is no rationale for indicting Arthur Andersen. That makes me throw–up.

Because, it is nearly impossible to convict executives on fraud charges (and they know that), and because, the laws are either non–existent or vague and hard to interpret—and expensive to prosecute and written by lawyers, for the oligarchs, and executives have the right to refuse to answer questions—or takes the Fifth, and complexity of these cases, and the ability of lawyers to convince at least one gullible—or bias juror of reasonable doubt—to nullify the trial; then, when they do convict—make verdicts stick, because, once they are rendered—the appeal process begins: and those with millions do not stop—until some judge caves in. By checking the record: I think, will prove–that corporate executives are seldom investigated and prosecuted—where complaints are made, unless there is strong public—outrage and once convicted—very few serve out their sentence—before they are sprung on an alleged error in the legal proceedings—or technicality—by some sympathetic judge.

This can be seen in the trial of Richard Scrushy, CEO of HealthSouth, charged with receiving $249 million linked to fraud and receiving in addition: 2.8 million shares of HealthSouth worth $15 million in a 58 count indictment and the twelve jurors were unable—to reach a unanimous verdict. It may have been more than they could handle—or some were bias. Unfortunately, juries do not always get it right, for example: OJ, Robert Blake, the first Menendez Brothers trial, the first Rodney King—police beating trial, the first trial of Kozlowski and Swartz looting Tyco International of $600 million. Their defense: the executives believed they acted lawfully when accepting forgiveness for company loans and spent Tyco's money (on personal things). The jury got it right the second time around. They plan to appeal. One thing, convicted executives have in common: they all deny wrongdoing.

The Supreme Court is a not–too–bright pack of two women and seven men—led by Rehnquist: loyal to the plundering plutocracy (not the people)—and displayed their utter contempt—for the victims of fraud and injustice.

Here are seven types of US obstructions of justice:

- 1: We know that Kenneth Lay, founder of Enron, and Vice President Cheney had meetings. We don't know what they discussed—or if, politicians were in anyway at fault in the Enron scandal. Because, keeping these things secret: is called: "executive privilege". Therefore, there is blackout at the highest level of government.

- 2: The deliberate physical destruction of documents that are self–incriminating—like in the Anderson case: is not criminal—according to Rehnquist. That is the voice of Satan.

- 3: The right of executives to take the Fifth—keep secret their company operations from the shareholders and government.

- 4: Because, big corporations own the mass media: radio and TV stations, newspapers, and magazines: they determine what news is reported and what is not.

- 5: Even if, members of the oligarchs are convicted—they, probably, will be sprung by the US courts (on some specious reason). For example: Andersen was over zealously prosecuted.

- 6: The US government—investigation and prosecution—of white–collar (or corporate) crime—in a bias matter.

- 7: It is illegal to take the law in your own hands—even if, you are a victim of fraud or crime—and the government ignores it.

Back in the Middle Ages kings and noblemen lived in castles with thick stonewalls, surrounded by a moot with a drawbridge and protected by portcullis. Today—we have a legal system that protects politicians and executives: and makes unethical enrichment by executives legal: that is their fortress (the codified legal system). And political donations help. What all these executives, who receive preferential treatment from the courts, have in common: Keating, Milken, Andersen, Keller, Barbakow, Brown, Sutherlin, Grubman, Wyle, et al; they are big contributors to political campaigns. Here are two cases placed side by side:

CASE A: Robert Whiteside—executive at Columbia/HCA convicted of defrauding Medicare, Medicaid, and CHAMPUS—of $645,796: sentenced to 2 years and pay restitution.

CASE Z: Leandro Andrade—a poor man—steals $153 worth of videos: at two different K–marts—pay restitution and sentenced to 50 years to life—and there are 300 more cases like him in California: serving 25 years to life—for petty theft—on the third strike.

Breaking news

2005 June 21: Rigas, CEO of the Adelphia Communications, was sentenced to 15 years—and his son, Timothy, 20 years: they were convicted of stealing: $100 million—and found guilty of conspiracy, securities and bank fraud: each equal to a felony or worst (because of the amount involved). And there were fifteen counts on securities fraud. Andrade got more time for two misdemeanors. Rigas denies wrongdoing and both plan to appeal.

Kozlowski and Swartz both were convicted—in the second trial—of stealing $150 million from Tyco and were convicted on 22 of 23 counts of grand larceny, conspiracy, securities fraud, and falsifying records. Sentencing is set for August. They deny wrongdoing and plan to appeal.

Ebbers was convicted of $11 billion of fraudulent bookkeeping at WorldCom—and nine counts of conspiracy, securities fraud, and filing false reports with regulators. He has not been sentenced yet, and plans to appeal. He also denies wrongdoing.

The Supreme Court nixing of the Andersen conviction—means: he is no longer a felon (after serving a coupe years on probation)—and can get his Certified Public Accounting firm licenses back—with a long "history of bad acts". He also claims to be innocent. Because, the management—of Andersen—violated its founder's motto—by refusing to "think straight and talk straight"—in its auditing practices and at the trial—taking the Fifth—it—doesn't deserve its Public Certification back. But, the Supreme Court's ruling—did just that. It set free a devious and unrepentant auditor. Enron was the biggest bankruptcy in US history at time: add to that: WorldCom, the Savings and Loans scandal, Qwest, etc.

What the Supreme Court Anderson ruling means: regardless of whether the jury's verdict was right—if the judge's instructions are wrong—the verdict should be overturned. I believe—that determine whether the jury's verdict was right—is far more important, then, determining whether the judge used the right terminology in his instructions to the jurors.

Judge—would you take a look at fifty flaws in the Andersen ruling.

Flaw # 1: According to Rehnquist: the faulty instructions allowed the jury to convict Andersen without proving the firm knew it broke the law. You see, how ridiculous that is. That would be a flaw—if, the evidence pointed to the fact: this was a routine disposal of old documents—not to impede a SEC investigation. Then, a person might be convicted for destroying old, useless documents. But, that was not the case—with Arthur Andersen. His partners seen the investigation coming and the shedding took place to thwart the investigation. The evidence was overwhelming—and plainly stated in the Grand Jury Charges—and indictment, which apparently—the justices failed to read.

Flaw # 2: Let's say: the four–foot bar represents the level of the burden of proof to convict: the judge lower it to three, but it does not matter: because the evidence cleared the bar by six feet.

Flaw # 3: that minor errors, or technicalities—are more important: than, whether the verdict was right or wrong.

Flaw # 4: the flaw in the jury instructions cited by Rehnquist—is irrelevant, because, the likelihood—of Arthur Andersen or top–level management not knowing what they did was wrong—is non–existent.

Flaw # 5: the flaw in the jury instructions cited by Rehnquist—is weak; because, what a person does—is a better proof of intent—than, what a person says he believes—faced with prosecution.

Flaw # 6: The flaw in the jury instructions cited by Rehnquist—is irrelevant: because Nancy Temple, Andersen's in–house lawyer and senior officers—took the Fifth—never testified under oath.

Flaw # 7: The jury instructions are more important—than, the evidence of evil intent. Since, Arthur Andersen is a firm—and not a person: and the top officers—refused to testify—the only way proof of intent can be demonstrated: is by what its partners—did. When—they seen the investigation coming: they deliberately shredded tons of Enron document—working overtime—to complete the task in time. This—is proof of evil intent (i.e., obstruct justice).

Flaw # 8: The evidence so compelling—this conviction—should never have been overturned on an irrelevant flaw in the jury instructions.

Flaw # 9: It is a subversion of justice.

Flaw # 10: The courts ruling—may have a negative impact on the over 100 civil suits pending. That, probably, was partly behind the ruling: making it harder to win these cases.

Flaw # 11: The court's ruling—is a hindrance to corporate fraud investigation and prosecution—rather than helpful. Frank F. Quattrone, an investment banker, convicted of similar charges—thinks: the overturn of the Andersen conviction will help his appeal—or others think.

Flaw # 12: the Supreme Court committed a legal crime—voiding the conviction of the most defiled auditor in US history.

Flaw # 13: It sends a wrong message to corporate looters.

Flaw # 14: It wasted taxpayers' money and resources.

Flaw # 15 Rehnquist's—opinion—that what one believes—is more important than what one does. There only two ways to prove intent (since it is a mind force; i.e., invisible)—is too ask a person his intent. Secondly: determine—his intent by what he does. We know what Andersen did—he destroyed tons of documents to obstruct an investigation: that is indisputable.

Flaw # 16: that the Supreme Court was either ignorant, corrupt, or dishonest—to believe that the shredding of the Enron documents could have been a routine disposal of old, unnecessary Enron documents—and those that approved and orchestrated it—were not conscious of wrongdoing.

Flaw # 17: that the deletion of this—so–called flaw—in the jury instructions—would have changed the outcome of the trial. Not—likely. Making the flaw inconsequential.

Flaw # 18: the so–called flaw—the overly broad instructions: is (somewhat) justified here; because, Andersen destroyed documents and refused to cooperate and testify—they did every thing they could—to subvert justice. It was necessary to make sure this—not straight thinking, not talking—corrupt auditing tax–consulting firm did not get away with the obstruction of justice. That seems to anger the Supreme Court.

Flaw # 19: the so–called faulty jury instructions—does not outweigh the tons of evidence—pointing to guilt.

Flaw # 20: Rehnquist based his ruling on the flawed jury instructions; but, the Oscar Criner, the jury foreman, said after the trial: "the jury instructions, didn't matter"—that undermines his argument.

Flaw # 21 The court set a bad precedent—by its ruling.

Flaw # 22: the ruling turned a just conviction—into an unjust exoneration of a felon: guilty of identity theft, witness tampering, and involvement in ten major strikes (accounting frauds: including Enron).

Flaw # 23 the court exonerated Andersen—while the firm continues to defy its founder's motto: by not talking. It does not deserve release from probation and reinstatement as a Public Certified auditor.

Flaw # 24: Rehnquist argued—the deletion of the word—dishonestly—as defining corruptly—from the instructions made it is too easy to convict: this is an error in the understanding of the law—or they way it is written—or intended. Knowingly is all that is required—if referring to causing someone to destroy or alter—evidence to obstruct an official proceeding. If, you do that: that is the definition of—corrupt persuasion: the person destroying the documents is not conscious of wrongdoing, but the persuader does. Rehnquist argues, argues, and argues—to make an invalid point—like a fool. The word—"Corruptly"—is superfluous. You're just as guilty, if you persuade, instruct, order, intimidate, coerce, or even attempt to so.

Flaw # 25: the ruling is so bad; the Supreme Court must to have been pressured by the government—or an oligarch: could it be: the National Association of Criminal Defense Lawyers (backing the Andersen appeal).

Flaw # 26: The chief justice Rehnquist is mentally flawed: he characterized the actions of Andersen: akin to: "a mother who suggests to her son that he invoke the right against compelled self–incrimination." He is taking the side of the criminal—against confession. This is the voice of Satan. He should be prosecuted for corrupting the youth of America. Would Rehnquist take this view—if, this boy—hid a bomb in the Supreme Court Building—and was to go off in 30 minutes and the FBI was interrogating him—should he holdout. Rehnquist—says: yes.

Flaw # 27: the flaw is not so much in the judge's instructions—as it is the in the way the law is written: it should be rewritten: to state: whoever, knowingly, persuades, uses his authority, or orders a person or employee to destroy—or alter documents—to obstruct an official investigation shall be fined (or guilty). That is a definition of "Corruptly persuades."

Flaw # 28: Rehnquist ruling is based one of six types of obstruction in the US Code: corrupt persuasion. But, it can be knowingly uses intimidation: I would think if, your boss ordered you to do something—that is intimidating: the employee—does not need to be conscious of wrongdoing. The boss does.

Flaw # 29: I believe Andersen—is guilty of corrupt persuasion: using their retention policy—as a disguise—to order the destruction of documents—to impede a government investigation of Enron and their own anticipated investigation. The law states an official proceeding—it had begun at Enron (and they were notified). And they had Enron pertinent documents.

Flaw # 30: the courts—used the intent factor—to overturn Keating's conviction: why not use the intent of the law—to reaffirm the conviction of Andersen: the indictment states: this was an unprecedented shredding of documents—not routine. The intent of law: knowingly is only required.

Flaw # 31: the ruling was wrong—because, the Supreme Court argued on the less likely side: there are only two:

ONE: the Andersen partners and senior officers did not know a SEC investigation was looming and this was a routine shredding of old Enron related documents. That is like, believing in Big Foot.

TWO: the partners and senior officers did know a SEC investigation was looming and they destroyed Enron related documents to thwart an investigation. This is what: justice Scalia—calls a "weird" government theory. He has got it backwards.

►Flaw # 32: the real flaws in this trial is not the judge's instructions—but, some of the jurors—they did not weigh the evidence correctly: the wholesale, frenetic, and worldwide destruction of documents and the confession of David B. Duncan—was by far more ponderous than the Oct. 16th Temple e–mail: knowing, this to be the truth—the conviction should have been reinforced.

Flaw # 33: the US Justice Department—did not put up an effective argument to block—the overturn of the Andersen conviction—or stand up for the victims of corporate white–collar crime.

Flaw # 34 the ruling—is a Supreme Court (legal) crime.

Flaw # 35: Rehnquist quotes about ten court cases—to support his arguments, which are lame and baseless.

Flaw # 36: because the Andersen conviction was hanging on a thread—instead of a rope: the Supreme Court should have fortified it, and instead cut it—until certain partners (or officers)—subject themselves to cross–examination under oath and reveal the full truth.

Flaw # 37: the addition of the word—impede to the instructions—Rehnquist states is overly broad. He is grasping at straws. Impede is a definition of obstruct in the Webster's dictionary.

Flaw # 38: Rehnquist objects to the use of the word: impede—with broad connotations; but, stretches the word corrupt—to mean evil, which connotes: murder, mayhem, Hitler, etc. He is inconsistent.

Flaw # 39: the fact, the Supreme Court to did not find the arguments of the petitioner—absurd. Nobody believes this was a routine disposal of old Enron related documents—except Andersen and the Supreme Court.

Flaw # 40 the ruling did not find that the US Justice Department put up a faint–hearted attempt to win this case—or break it open. The reason: the head of SEC, Harvey Pitt, was a former Andersen lawyer (and probably), did not want to go after his former boss, friends, and co–workers.

Flaw # 41: the fact, the Supreme Court to did not find the arguments of the defense at the trial—an attempt to twist the facts—and delude the jury—and that is why, they agreed only on one count.

Flaw # 42: the law does not require the destruction be done—by corrupt persuasion. It can be by intimidation. Instructions from a superior—or WO to an employee—are very intimidating (one could be fired, etc). It is corrupt persuasion; because, the Temple first email was called: the company's document retention policy. When, it was—a disguise—for the company's destruction policy (of incriminating evidence). It corruptly persuaded its employees.

Flaw # 43: the ruling—sounds like Rehnquist is acting as the defense attorney for the petitioner. He falsely argues. He argues biasly. He uses legal jargon, etc. He does not use common sense.

Flaw # 44: the ruling argues to vindicate Andersen—as if—he was wrongly convicted—and the shredding was legal. The truck drivers and operators of the shredders—probably, were not conscious of wrongdoing; but the Andersen partners–or senior officers ordering it (to avoid civil litigation and criminal prosecution)—were. There was no emergency—to dump old documents. The emails (or files) on computers—pose no storage problem. Generally, it is wise to keep them—as proof—what was said (or done).

Flaw # 45 the ruling was uninformed of the facts.

►Flaw # 46 Rehnquist states: the act of persuasion—standing alone: "is by itself innocuous" but, it does not stand by itself—it is part of a sentence. You can delete both <u>knowingly</u> and <u>corruptly</u>—(from the sentence—and you still have the definition of a corrupt persuader. You mean—to say: who-ever persuades a person (or employee)—to destroy or alter documents to obstruct an official investigation—is not breaking the law. Rehnquist is an ignoramus.

Flaw # 47: the ruling opens up the gate to fraud.

Flaw # 48: the ruling focused on less than 1% of the trial and ignores more than 99%. Rehnquist eyes are bad—he has tunnel vision.

Flaw # 49: the ruling is a corrupt argument—and falsely raises the bar of proof: that corrupt persuasion is necessary: it is not—the way it is written in the US code—referring to what the rest of the sentence is referring to. Cor-ruptly is redundant: the same as knowingly. Here is what Rehnquist said: "The outer limits of this element need not be explored here because the jury instructions at issue simply failed to convey the requisite consciousness of wrongdoing. Indeed, it is striking how little culpability the instructions required. For example, the jury was told that, 'even if [petitioner] honesty and sincerely believed that its conduct was lawful, you may find [petitioner] guilty."

Of course, you can—if, you think the person is lying. He is relying on the person's belief—as more reliable proof—than, the facts. First—they lied: and second: they took the Fifth. It is the same, if, a person pleads not guilty—and he sincerely believes it—then, you cannot convict. He is nuts. The Andersen partners or senior officers were well aware of the law and they tried wiggled around it. They did not wiggle—they ran through road barriers. Do you think—these lawyers—and partners—who have been through this many times: did not know that destroying evidence—needed in a legal proceeding violated the law. I bet, they felt sudden fright, when the SEC announced the investigation. They tried to beat the law—by destroying evidence, falsely testifying, and taking the Fifth. Duncan—first lied, and took the Fifth—and later confessed.

Rehnquist—biggest contradiction: he does not believe Duncan's confession. He believes those that took the Fifth. Duh.

Flaw # 50: Andersen violated the intent of the law—by not making Enron documents available—for an official proceeding: and the Supreme Court's ruling: defended them. The Andersen and its top officers instructed employees to destroy Enron document: knowing—that the government begun an investigation—into the Enron scandal—and their involvement. This prompted the quick document shredding and purging of computer files and is an obstruction of justice.

Let's review the evidence—again:

Joseph F. Berardino—the CEO of Andersen—fights a Grand Jury investigation and indictment, and makes misleading statements....

It also might be in violation of a signed cease and desist order from the SEC (not to engage in future securities–law violations)—rising from their audits of Waste Management, Inc. Temple's handwritten note of phone call with her boss on Oct. 9th says: "Highly probable SEC inquiry".

Michael C. Odom—Andersen's partner at Houston knew Enron was headed for big trouble—for months. And on Oct. 9, 2001 hired a firm law to prepare a defense—for events soon to unfold. Enron was in the first stages of a meltdown—and Andersen auditors knew it.

On Oct. 10—Michael C. Odom told 89 employees about the firm's document retention policy at training meeting: he said:

"If it's destroyed in the course of normal policy, and litigation is filed the next day, that's great.... We've followed our own policy, and whatever there was that might have been of interest to somebody is gone and irretrievable": here is your corrupt persuader. He is trying to deceive employees they are doing nothing wrong—by destroying Enron document. He is preparing them for this task—in a deceitful way.

Two days later:

10/12/2001: Nancy B Duncan, in house–lawyer at Andersen's headquarters at Chicago: E–mails Michael C Odom, at Huston's office: subject: Document retention policy: it states: "Mike—"It might be useful to consider reminding the engagement team of our documentation and retention policy. It will be helpful to make sure that we have complied with this policy. Let me know if you have any questions". This is the first get–ready alert from Andersen's headquarters—not on retention—but destruction.

The same morning: Michael C. Odom: forwards the email to David B. Duncan, head of the Enron auditing team. The email is using the company's retention policy as—**a disguise**—for the company's destruction of incriminating evidence—policy. It "corruptly persuades". It also is intimidating: coming from Andersen's headquarters and partners.

Retention policy ◄► (destroy)

Before the massive destruction of Enron related documents—was launched—by Houston partners: it already started—on a small scale. Temple verbally told various employees: to follow the company's document retention policy: they began destroying documents and deleting emails in their offices.

Just two day later after the bad news release: Enron notified Anderson: the SEC had begun in investigation into its accounting procedures. Then, David B. Duncan: orders the immediate and systematic destruction of tons of documents pertaining to Enron.

TWINS

The difference between Odom and Duncan: one refuses to testify: the other confesses: both are guilty—in my opinion. They were Andersen partners at Houston. Odom was over Duncan: the Nancy Temple email came to Odom who sent it to Duncan. Duncan could not have carried out this massive destruction of Enron related documents without authorization. Duncan maintains he was following company orders.

To prove the retention policy was really their destruction policy: in a Oct. 24 memo from a manager, employees were told the document shredding was so important that it should be pursued even: "on an overtime basis, if necessary for the remainder of this week or for however long it takes." This is no routine disposal of nonessential documents.

October 25: Enron sends an email—to Andersen: stating all pertinent documents should be preserved. The shredding continued to until November 9th—when they were handed a SEC subpoena—to provide

Enron documents. It, not only, violated the law; because, they were notified beforehand, that the government had begun an official investigation, but, it violated its clients email to preserve documents. This cannot be the retention policy of a Public Certified auditor. The indictment—states: never happened before like this.

If, you take a look at the second e–mail: it specifically states in detail: what the company's document retention policy is. If, that was sent the first time: there would be no shredding of documents. The first email—was non–specific (you know what I mean email). For legal reasons—it was not stated in clear terms. What it meant—can be determine by what they did.

There are least four corrupt persuaders:

1. **Joseph Berardino————CEO?**

2. David B. Duncan: he confessed.

3. Michael Odom: he took the Fifth

4. Thomas Bauer: he took the Fifth

5. Nancy Temple: she took the Fifth

6. And there are others.............

▶**The one in–house lawyer at the Chicago Headquarters and two Houston partners that took the Fifth—are the big obstructers of justice—in the Arthur Andersen LLP trial.**

June 2002: Twelve jurors unanimously convicts Andersen: on one count of witness tampering (or obstruction of justice).

The conviction was upheld by the 5th District Court of Appeals.

—Two years later: The Supreme Court—voids the guilty verdict—on flimsy, falsely argued flaws in the trial judge's instructions.

—This ruling—voids the Grand Jury charges and indictment.

—This ruling—voids—the ruling of the 5th District Court of Appeals—upholding the conviction.

—The ruling—disregards the statement of the acting Assistant Attorney General John C. Richer: that the Justice Department had charged Andersen because of its: "determination that the substantial destruction of documents in anticipation an investigation by the Securities and Exchange Commission violated the law".

The US government investigation, prosecution, and subsequent overturn of Andersen's conviction was flawed and politically motivated—because: Andersen was a big donor to Bush and members of congress (political campaigns)—and Harvey Pitt, a former Andersen lawyer—appointed by Bush as the director of SEC—who was the leader of the anti–Levitt effort—to banish cozy relationships between auditors and executives—in the late 1990s: the white house—SEC nexus, and Antonin Scalia, who derided the Andersen prosecution—is a sleep–in–buddy with Bush—at the white house. They are all members of the ruling oligarchs—even Supreme Court is tainted. This can be seen by their corrupt ruling—overturning the Andersen verdict—a big supporter of Bush and former auditor of Halliburton.

The Attorney General, Alfredo Gonzales, appointed by Bush—has said: nothing (critical—that I know of). He is a dud.

Conclusion

In conclusion: Supreme Court ruling—was multi–flawed—misanalysed, wrong, full of holes, false arguments, illogical, a hodge–podge of nonsense, an incorrect and deceitful presentation of facts, over the head of the people, overlooks a mountain of evidence, a misinterpretation of the US code, and a big setback of the government's crack down on corporate crime. It is cockeyed—almost in its entirety, and should be flushed down the toilet.

My last Judgment

My last ruling: The Supreme Court should be prosecuted for partiality, incompetence, subverting justice—and aiding the corporate looters—convicted and put in stocks for one week—for public ridicule—fined $10,000, and sentenced to 1 year in jail (for voiding a guilty conviction—by corrupt persuasion). Today, (some) executives and politicians—are no better than those beheaded in France. People who knowing by fraud—destroys the life–savings of hundreds and thousands of people—should be executed.

For example: the executive who told employees who have Enron shares in their 401k retirement accounts—that the corporation was viable and would come back, while executives sold their shares (in a falling market). This is a capital offense. I might modify the death sentence—if, they had the ability to repay.

In the US—a lot of corporate fraud is legal—sanctioned and protected by the Supreme Court—that is it alright to depose of incriminating evidence to obstruct an investigation and prosecution—like Arthur Andersen did—which Rehnquist describes as—acting like the mother advising her son. But, the US Justice Department—is not supposed to be like Andersen's mother. And the relationship between Andersen and its employees—is not mother and son. If, you're going to use an analogy use one that is analogous. The employees have not committed the crime: it is Andersen telling his employees—to destroy evidence of a crime he has committed—or Enron.

And Andersen is not the mother of Enron—they are more like—co–conspirators: that is why, they both destroyed documents. Rehnquist goes on to write: It "is not inherently malign" to persuade someone to withhold documents from the government. It is, if someone is suspected of committing a crime. I believe that is the case—here. He opened up a crack. He is a supreme judicial crackpot.

———————————

Parents should decide

Not long ago: I entered a public library and the room where the computers are—and I found to my astonishment—that a number of children were watching porn on the computers. And I went to the librarian and told her. She said: we know, but, there is nothing we can do. Because, the Supreme Court has ruled it is their First Amendment right.

Like, the writers of the Bill of Rights—envisioned computers and the Internal—and ordained—beforehand—it is the right of your children to enter public libraries and view pornography.

Thanks to the Supreme Court—they can.

978-0-595-36670-5
0-595-36670-8